FOREX
FOR SMALL
SPECULATORS

12/24/2008

To Wilson,
Good luck & good
fortune in trading
Robert Drakoln

FOREX
FOR SMALL
SPECULATORS

For investors with
$1,000 to $15,000 of risk capital

By
Noble DraKoln

FOREX FOR SMALL SPECULATORS

For information, address

Enlightened Financial Press
404 E. First St. # 1396
Long Beach, CA 90802

ISBN 0-9666245-8-0

To my family
Ann, Alex, and Zach
Without whom none of this would be possible

TABLE OF CONTENTS

Introduction

Part One

Thank you very much for reading this installment of the Small Speculators™ series. Like the first book, **Futures For Small Speculators,** I have written this book because I want potential investors to fully understand what foreign exchange (forex) is all about. Small speculators are flocking in droves to this exciting new opportunity, but they are coming unprepared.

I have not gone in to great depth on what the best technical indicators are, nor do I explain various sure-fire ways to make "millions". As a licensed professional in the futures business, I feel it is neither necessary nor appropriate. What I focus on in this book is the necessary attitude and tools you need to have in order to make trading an enjoyable experience, whether you are winning or losing. If you don't enjoy what you do, simply because you are frustrated, you will give up before you can succeed at it.

Free-floating currencies have only been around for a little over thirty years. From the beginning, currencies have been traded in two forms, "over-the-counter" (OTC) cash trading and exchange-traded currency futures and options.

For twenty five years only super-high net worth individuals and banks could obtain the necessary credit to trade the OTC currencies. Five key factors changed all of that and leveled the OTC playing field. First, the introduction of the Internet. This changed the way major banks and dealers handled orders and risk management. Second, in 2000 we saw the introduction of the Commodity Futures

Modernization Act which changed the rules and regulations for futures and leveraged investing. Third, we saw the introduction of the euro as a new currency. Fourth was the wide acceptance of online investing and banking by consumers. Lastly, the recent introduction of "mini" accounts from OTC currency dealers. All of this has created a speculative renaissance for forex trading that has also spilled over into exchange traded currencies.

Forex trading, whether OTC or futures, is very exciting. What makes it so exciting as a great speculative investment is the amount of leverage you are allowed. Forex futures can have a leverage ratio of 10 to 1, or more. On the other hand, OTC forex can have leverage ratios as high as 100 to 1. While leverage is a double-edged sword, this tremendous leverage can make minor fluctuations in currency prices seem tremendous to the bottom line of profits and, more importantly, losses.

All forex trading must be given a lot of respect. While many approach forex with a gambler's mentality, the real key to succeeding in forex is being a competent speculator.

My favorite definition of speculation is "to engage in risky business transactions on the chance of generating great profits". Speculation is not gambling. Gambling generally involves pure chance and blind luck. Forex is based on the currencies of countries with real issues of trade surpluses or deficits, change in interest rates, and economic stability or instability. Forex speculators must strategize, research, and plan if they ever hope to understand what is happening on such a large macroeconomic scale.

Today, small speculators with as little capital as US$500 to put at risk can become players in the forex arena, although I typically recommend between $2,500 and $15,000 if you want longevity.

Even with such a low cost to enter, forex speculation is not suitable for everyone. Forex is a fast moving market that operates 24 hours a day, six days a week. You can rake in losses just as fast as your profits. This aspect of forex trading can be very stressful and taxing on the psyche. For many, the challenge of trading a 24- hour market is definitely an allure. Just be careful of liking the challenge so much you miss sight of the goal: profits.

The ability to trade whenever you want catches new forex speculators off guard. They begin to trade when fatigued. Fatigued traders make lots of mistakes. Losses mount quickly and it becomes harder to make the right decisions.

Small speculators, in general, often get caught in a perpetual cycle of losing. The small speculator may read something in the newspaper that looks like a sure-fire trade. The small speculator then hypes himself up about how much money he can make. He then executes the trade without any strategy, research, or planning. The small speculator "gambles" his money away. Then he does the same thing all over again in another month or two. The attitude quickly becomes "it's only $500".

If you find yourself in any of these situations or think that you have a personality that predisposes you to fall into any of these traps, forex speculation may not be for you.

In order to give yourself a fair chance of success in forex trading, you must avoid the behaviors mentioned above and behave like your professional dealer and bank counterparts.

Part Two

Currencies have existed in some form or another for thousands of years. Whether they were shells, beads, or gold, people have always used some medium of exchange to assist in bartering services and goods.

Futures have been traded all around the world for centuries as well. Similar to insurance they have been used to shift the risk from both the buyers and sellers to the speculator. Speculators have always been the merchant bankers of necessity.They provide the capital that both the buyers and the sellers need in order to make futures an effective risk management tool.The buyers and the sellers of currencies could never afford to make a mistake if they didn't have futures to back up their trading decisions.

When companies promote forex they typically focus only on the OTC cash market. This is limiting. Because forex trading exists in two forms simultaneously, the OTC cash market and the futures market, small speculators have access to a lot of the same capabilities as large banking institutions. This is a unique scenario not found in many other investment opportunities.

Being able to trade both markets simultaneously puts you on par with hedgers, even when speculating. This is a one-of-a-kind situation that creates all of sorts of interesting speculative opportunities.

Large speculators, hedge funds and investment groups, see this opportunity and actually trade both sides of forex with ease. They also realize that there isn't an easy way to predict the direction of the OTC forex market, although you can rely on the market movement once it picks a direction. They also realize that all forex trading is a zero-sum game. Any money they lose is won by someone else.

With all of this in mind, large speculators have realized that disciplined trading requires that they explore all of their options. This is the only way in which they can succeed. As a small speculator, you will have to be just as disciplined, if not more disciplined than your large speculator counterparts.

The first key to that discipline is being willing to prepare for the losing trades. Many small speculators will put all of their limited risk capital behind one trade. Many more will add to losing trades. Some of them will actually try to fight against the market. Try to avoid these traps.

The second key is to prepare for your winning trades. In forex, don't be afraid to lock in the profits from a winning trade with a futures or options forex contract. You never want to be caught in a currency reversal and give back profits.

The third key is to have faith in yourself and your decision-making process. Don't wait for your sure-fire trade to prove itself and miss out on all the profits by picking the top of a market.

Every preventable mistake is rooted in two emotions, "fear" and "greed". Small speculators consistently react with either one of these emotions, setting themselves up for failure by leaving no room for discipline.

So, why aren't small speculators disciplined?

The answer: There has never been a book like this that specifically focuses on the needs of the small speculator.

Part Three

This brings us back to why I had to write this book. I have been involved with futures for the past eleven years. I was first introduced to forex trading in 1997. During this time I have been a broker's assistant, a broker, an investor, a seminar speaker and a futures and forex brokerage firm owner. I have dealt with hundreds of small speculators, each of them wanting the same thing, the greatest profits from their limited resources.

First hand experience has taught me three things: 1) small speculators do not truly understand the mechanics of forex, 2) small speculators do not know the various types of ways they can get involved with forex, and 3) small speculators do not see what mistakes are preventable.

First, let me tell you what this book is not. This book is not a Holy Grail of system trading. This book does not discuss technical analysis, fundamental analysis, or any permutation thereof in depth. Nor does this book teach you how to never lose money speculating on forex.

Now let me tell you what this book is. It is a good resource for the beginning forex speculator. This book is a reference guide for the experienced small speculator. This book is to be used in conjunction with any and all trading systems that you may be using now. This book was written to reinforce the things you may be doing right and to help you overcome the things that you may be doing wrong.

This book is divided into three sections. Section one is a basic explanation of forex, including case studies. Section two discusses the various forex trading arenas. Section three breaks down all of the common, preventable mistakes that small speculators make.

Ultimately, this book was written to help small speculators navigate between the demons of fear and greed, all the while knowing how and why they made or lost money. There is also a glossary section at the end of this volume that details any terms with which you may be unfamiliar.

Thank you for purchasing my book and I wish you much success in all of your speculative investing.

Noble A. DraKoln

Section One:

Fundamentals
of Foreign Exchange

Foreign Exchange *n. Abbr.* **Forex or FX**

1. Transaction of international monetary business, as between governments or businesses of different countries.
2. Negotiable bills drawn in one country to be paid in another country.

The American Heritage® Dictionary of the English Language, Fourth Edition Copyright © 2000 by Houghton Mifflin Company.

Chapter One
The History of Forex

The Forex trading market is a relatively new phenomenon. Never before in the history of the world have we seen such an amazing event. In only 30 years, this industry has developed from almost nothing to a daily US$1.5 trillion market. How did this happen? Was it by design? Or was it by accident?

Well the answer falls somewhere in between. There are three distinct time frames that set the stage for today's style of currency trading. The first time frame is the pre-currency trading era of the 1950's. The second time frame is the worldwide, politically volatile atmosphere of the 1970's. The third time frame is what has occurred in this free market economy since the demise of the gold standard 30 years ago. In each time frame, there have been three catalysts: war, gold, and foreign banks- that have played a significant role in propelling currency development.

Pre-Currency Trading Era – 1950's

Entering into the 1950's, the United States of America had a distinct advantage over war-torn Europe. While Germany was heavily sanctioned, England, France, Italy, and several other Old World nations were just coming to terms with the heavy investment needed to rebuild their countries.

As a way to make it easier for the rest of the world to rebuild, the Bretton Woods Agreement was adopted. It was innocuously simple: in an effort to keep the United States of America (USA) from buying everything in sight, the Bretton Woods Agreement kept the USA in check by requiring all foreign currencies be pegged to the US Dollar. Some pegs were strong, some pegs were weak, but at the end of the day they never moved more than 1% in any direction. Like today's problem with the Chinese Yuan, forced to a peg against the dollar, it kept a constant, controlled flow of US dollars out of the country.

The peg would not have been so bad if not for the fact that the US dollar also had a unique relationship with gold. Just like currencies, gold was pegged to the dollar at a fixed value of US$35/ounce. What made it even worse was that US currency, at the time, was directly exchangeable for gold. This strategy was fine as long as the Fort Knox gold reserves exceeded $23 billion.

After World War II, the USA became the primary economic super power. Many foreign countries began to acquire US currency in lieu of gold. The dollar gained prominence in a way no other currency ever had before.

At the same time, we began to see the rebuilding of the Old World and foreign trade began to gain momentum. In 1950, foreign countries held US $8 billion. We also saw the oil business begin its ascent as a prominent import/export industry.

1970's United States Currency Policy Meltdown

Once again, we are hit with the triumvirate of war, the restrictive gold standard, and dollars in foreign banks.

This time, each problem was feeding directly off of the others. The Vietnam Conflict had drained our gold reserves heavily. By 1970, Fort Knox only held US$12 Billion.

The growth of the oil business and with the increase in foreign trade caused a boom in the demand for US dollars in foreign banks. Over US$ 47 Billion was sitting in overseas banks.

On paper, our gold reserves were over-leveraged by almost 4 to 1. As a nation, we did not know how to react to such an overbearing assault on our currency. Then along came the invention of the Eurodollar to make our nightmare worse.

Foreign banks with US dollars would make low-interest loans in US dollars to importers and exporters. Although the dollars were never repatriated, the US was still on the hook to exchange these "credit"-created dollars for the gold we kept on reserve.

Then came a miracle in disguise . The Bretton Woods Agreement collapsed. In the over-leveraged gold-dollar environment, many countries began to feel frustrated with the artificial peg.

In blatant defiance to the agreement in 1971, Germany declared that they would float the Deutsche mark. They were tired of the artificial peg that was keeping their economy depressed.

In the first hour of trading, over US$1 billion were exchanged for Deutsche marks. For the first time, the public had voiced their opinion against being so heavily weighted with dollars.

With Germany completely ignoring the Bretton Woods Agreement by floating their currency, the US government had nothing left to do but put the final nail in the coffin of the U.S.'s currency policy. The Bretton Woods Agreement was dissolved.

Three short months after the Deutsche mark began to float, the US moved off of the gold standard. Gold was allowed to float freely like any other currency. Oil, although priced in US dollars, soon switched to a peg against gold. Gold and oil prices jumped ten-fold.

The currency dynamics were soon changed on a global scale and it became accepted practice that countries began to float their own currency.

New Rules of Currency

In 1971, the Smithsonian Agreement replaced the Bretton Woods Agreement and authorized "forward currency contracts", adding validity to the Eurodollar phenomenon. It didn't work. A year later the European Joint Float was established. It, and the Smithsonian Agreement, were scrapped in 1973. Even though they were dissolved the concept of "forward currency contracts" stayed as part of the banking system.

Once currencies began to "free-float", they immediately moved away from their gentlemanly 1% fluctuations on either side to huge price ranges, going anywhere from 20-25% daily.

From 1970-1973, the total foreign exchange volume went from US$25 Billion to US$100 Billion. With oil prices up, gold prices up, and an economy still reeling from the rapid currency shift, "stagflation", rising inflation while real incomes remained the same, soon hit the United States

Today's Currency World

In the 30 years since the collapse of the last gentlemanly agreement on currency rates, many momentous events have occurred that have affected currencies worldwide. The Japanese yen gained prominence because of Japan's heavy export relationship with the United States. The USSR collapsed. We have had several undeclared wars, the south Asian economies have risen and collapsed, and several investor bubbles have come and gone.

Each time, currencies have come away with a newly earned respect by the masses. There has also been a constant element of surprise that keeps you guessing what's next.

Current conditions, such as the United States' perpetual war on "terror", the permanent introduction and dominance of the euro currency, the steady O.P.E.C. increases in oil prices, and gold's renaissance as a store of value, will likely have a tremendous impact on the future of what it means to trade currencies.

This could be a fundamental shift in the next phase of currency development.

Chapter Two
Forex Mechanics

There are several important components to both the OTC and futures sides of forex trading. The only place they differ is in the type of participants and how their contracts are designed. Otherwise, the concepts of margin, types of positions and types of orders are very much the same.

OTC

The Participants

Banks and Dealers are the essential back-bone of the OTC markets. There is no central market place, so the banks and dealers provide credibility, liquidity, credit, and the price quotes. Without these two groups, there is no forex market.

Insurers and Corporations are large users of forex to settle their annuity, import, and export transactions. Their businesses dictate that each transaction is customized. With this customization they need the proper tools to protect themselves. The customized spot and forward contracts that forex can provide makes it convenient and flexible for their treasury departments to budget and plan.

Speculators. Forex has many famous speculators, from the famous, such as George Soros, to the infamous, such as Long Term Capital Management. The same banks and dealers that make markets for forex also trade for profits on their own account or on the behalf of their clients. Individuals now play a significant part in this 24-hour market.

Components of a custom contract

Spot contracts are settled two days after the deal date. They are very straight-forward in the various components of the contracts.

The Currency Pair system is the normal way that currencies are priced. The first quoted currency is known as the "base" currency. The second quoted currency is known as the "counter" or "quote" currency. You buy or sell a currency in relation to another currency. There are hard currencies which represent the G7 economies, such as the US dollar, the euro, and the Japanese yen. There are also currencies known as "softs", which represent the non-G7economies, such as the South African rand or the Romanian leu. Each currency price is listed in a five-number increment, of which only the last two numbers are quoted.

Currency spread is the difference between what the banks or dealer are willing to pay for a particular currency and at what price they are willing to sell a particular currency. This amount can have any range. The typical spread is 3 to 7 "pips or bps".

Bps also known as Pips in the forex industry are the units of increment that currency instruments are measured in. Depending on the currency, pips may have a value of approximately US$7 -$11.

Contract size is wholly customized by the trader. Depending on the size of the account, you will be able to trade contracts in the several hundred thousands or in the several millions. It depends solely on the amount of leverage you want.

Interest rates play a crucial factor in holding spot currency trades longer than two days. This is known as a "rollover". Since currencies are traded in pairs, subtract the interest you receive when selling another currency from the interest that you must pay to hold a currency, to find the interest you earn or are liable for past the two day spot trading period.

In the book, *Futures For Small Speculators,* I explain, in depth, all of the futures participants, as well as each component that makes up a futures contract.

Both OTC and futures forex markets share the following features in common:

Margin

Even though the OTC forex market uses margin, it is definitely more aggressive than futures.

First, I will give a brief explanation of margins associated with stocks. A stock investor places a cash down payment on shares and then borrows the difference from a broker to purchase the stocks.

This is not the case in the OTC and futures forex markets. In these markets margin money is simply considered earnest money.

As a trade unfolds, either more money is added to your account or money is deducted from your margin "earnest money".

The key difference between the OTC and futures market is the amount of money you must put up. In the faster OTC spot market, investors can get away with as little as 1% of the total currency value, a leverage ratio of 100 to 1. In the futures forex market the amounts are higher, more in the 5%-10% range, a leverage ratio of 20 to 1 or 10 to 1.

There are two types of earnest money margins: initial margin and maintenance margin. Initial margin is the earnest money you need to establish your position. Maintenance margin is the minimum amount of earnest money that can keep your trade active before you have a margin call or your trade is automatically closed out. Due to the high amounts of leverage available in OTC trading, the forex market has created safeguards that automatically close accounts that drop below the maintenance margin so that your account is never at a net deficit. This system is not found in futures.

Types of Positions

Long positions are the easiest to understand. They operate on the "buy low, sell high" philosophy. A trader initiates a trade by "buying" a contract. He offsets a trade by "selling" or shorting a contract.

Short positions are sometimes difficult for traditional stock traders to understand. In this scenario the goal is to "sell high, buy low". A trader "sells" a contract and later offsets it by "buying" it back.

Although there are currency options on OTC and futures forex contracts, as of this writing they don't play a significant role for retail investors. If you would like more in-depth details about them, e-mail us at currencyoptions@liverpoolgroup.com and I will send you a free report.

Types of Orders

A **Market order** is used when you want to get the order done immediately at the market price.

A **Limit order** is an order to buy at or below a limit price that you set or an order to sell at or above a limit price that you set. If the market is trading above a limit sell order when entered, it will act like a market order. If the market is trading below a limit buy order it will act like a market order. If the market is not trading at a favorable price, your order will not be executed.

A **Stop order** is used to buy above the market, or to sell below the market. Unlike a limit order, you are not guaranteed that the order will be filled at or better than your stop price. Stop orders are usually filled at a price worse than your stop price because the market is usually moving against you.

There are many more types of orders, but ninety percent of small speculators will only use these three.

Chapter Three
Broker Selection

In the OTC forex market, an ingrained culture of broker assisted trading has never developed. Many private traders learned their skills by working at a bank or for a hedge fund. They developed lines of credit for themselves and were on a first-name basis with dealer desks from London to Tokyo.

With the introduction of OTC forex trading for retail investors, there has been an emphasis on transaction price with no brokers to "get in the way". To the dismay of many novice and intermediate traders, the elimination of the broker has not saved them money, but actually cost them thousands in educational material. They attend seminars and buy books, like this one, to learn basic information that a broker would gladly give them for free.

Also, with the elimination of a broker it becomes difficult to use time- and money-saving strategies, simply because you do not become aware of them.

In futures, there has always been a licensed professional to turn to. Companies can benefit from having a broker that fully understands both the OTC and futures side of the forex market. When searching for assistance in trading the forex market, look to find a firm or private professional that combines these disciplines.

Several characteristics make a futures professional top-quality. Most importantly, he must be dedicated to making the "professional-client" team relationship work. A futures professional must be capable of monitoring your trades, have the experience to help you develop a trading plan, and be willing to be a personal coach who helps you navigate between the trading demons of fear and greed until you can trade on your own.

It is great to work with discount brokers, but you get what you pay for, which is typically an order taker. It doesn't matter whether you deal with them on the telephone or over the Internet. They do not catch incorrect trades, nor do they guide you in the development of a trading plan. They compete solely on price. Small speculators that rely solely on price will often find themselves with an extended learning curve.

Futures Professional Checklist

√   Available 8am-8pm
√   Thoroughly understands the OTC forex market
√   Is responsive and honest
√   Deals well with losses
√   Familiar with trading, has had a demo account at least
√   Believes in developing a trading plan
√   Encourages you to keep a trading journal
√   Has market experience
√   Has knowledge of the trading demons fear and greed
√   Has a positive track record with his clients
√   Has an open personality

√ Is reliable

√ Has a reasonable commission rate

Client Checklist

√ Make yourself accessible during the market hours of your trades

√ Have multiple contact numbers available for your futures professional

√ Know how to handle margin calls if you cannot be contacted

√ Know what will be considered a trading emergency

√ Know who to contact when you are not available

√ Have after hours contact information for your broker

√ A contact person who can act on your behalf in the event you are incapacitated.

√ Make provisions for unusual situations.

Chapter Four
Funding Your Account

Properly funding your account begins with you determining your net liquid assets (NLA). NLA includes all your assets that can be converted to cash within 24 hours. This includes savings accounts, CDs, common stocks, and other saleable securities.

Once your NLA has been determined, you can then set aside up to ten percent of this capital for speculative investing. For example, if an individual has net liquid assets of $50,000, the amount of speculative capital will be 10 percent, or $5,000.

Chapter Five
Forex Case Studies

Forex trading is a highly fast-paced venture that has only been around for about 30 years. Yet, in this time, many legendary currency events have unfolded. In this chapter we look at a few events that have had a tremendous impact on currencies and currency trading worldwide. Many of these events, because of the circumstances, will be either impossible to duplicate, or greatly surpassed in the future. What makes these events amazing is the fact that they happened at all. They serve as cautionary tales against being arrogant when trading forex. They also act as inspiration to give you a glimpse of great things that may come in the future of foreign exchange.

Case Study 1:

George Soros is the founder of the Quantum Fund. It is considered to be one of the world's first hedge funds. George Soros, unlike many investment managers, takes a macroeconomic view of investing. With this uncanny talent, he has successfully hunted down tremendously profitable investment opportunities around the world. In fact, in a few of the other case studies, George Soros, or his money management firm Quantum Fund, have played a significant role.

One investment led him to be considered a pariah in the United Kingdom and brought him both the admiration and disdain of many financiers worldwide.

George Soros had discerned that the British pound was top heavy. He felt that it was long overdue for a correction and that there was nothing the central bank could do to stop the currency from sliding downward. So George Soros began to build up a highly leveraged short position against the British pound. Over the course of six months, he racked up profits of over US$1 billion. This devastated the British pound and scandalized the government. Ever since then, George Soros has been known as the man that broke the Bank of England.

George Soros is also known for the active role he played in the Russian economy before the Russian government defaulted on their bonds 1998. The Russian ruble collapsed. At the time, George Soros was so vested in the Russian economy that he committed US$2 billion towards its success. He later lost all but a fraction of his investment due to Russia's economic collapse.

Case Study 2:

In late 1996 Asian countries were being noted globally for their unprecedented economic growth. Technology and manufacturing were large contributors to the new-found financial strength in Indonesia, Malaysia, Thailand, and Singapore. Export/import partners of these countries wondered how long their growth could be sustained. The main business attraction that had encouraged business in those countries in the first place, undervalued currencies, had gotten significantly stronger.

In early 1997, Soros' groups began heavily shorting Thailand's currency, the baht, and Malaysia's currency, the ringgit, using the same highly leveraged tactics as had been used five years earlier against the British pound.

In July of 1997, in order to stimulate their weakening economy, Thai officials devalued the baht. This action set off a wave of devaluations throughout Asia, most notably Malaysia. South Asia still has not successfully recovered from this aggressive currency attack.

Soros has said that when the government officials finally devalued the currencies his funds had already turned bullish. He claims he lost money as well when the values of the Thai and Malaysian currencies plummetted from their all time highs.

Prime Minister Mahathir Mohamad of Malaysia declared to the world his disdain for George Soros and his currency-crippling investment strategies.

Case Study 3:

Long-Term Capital Management (LTCM) was a hedge fund founded with Nobel Prize winners Myron Scholes and Robert Merton on the board.

LTCM had developed a trading style that utilized arbitrage. They focused their efforts on trading U.S., Japanese, and European sovereign bonds. The arbitrage focused on a simple concept: over time the value of long-dated bonds issued a short time apart would tend to become identical because the bonds that were trading at a premium would decrease in value and the bonds trading at a discount would increase in value. The profits between the two were practically guaranteed. This risk-free profit would become more and more apparent every time a new bond was issued.

Since the profit opportunity was "very" thin, LTCM needed more leverage than most companies in order to make the program worthwhile for their investors. In 1998, the firm started out with equity of US$4.72 billion. They used that equity to borrow over US$124.5 billion and leveraged assets of around $129 billion. They then used these positions to convince banks to give them off-balance-sheet derivative positions amounting to US$1.25 trillion.

Initially, this heavily leveraged strategy produced returns in the double digits. These "risk free" profits stopped in August 1998, when Russia defaulted on their sovereign debt. Investors lost faith in Japanese and European bonds. U.S. treasury bonds became the bonds of the hour. The expected bond narrowing not only stopped, but quickly began to diverge. LTCM lost US$1.85 billion in capital.

Because LTCM had daisy-chained so much leverage, if they failed, the effect would not only be a loss of capital, but a banking crisis to the tune of at least US$1.25 trillion.

To save the global economy, the Federal Reserve Bank of New York, without putting up any taxpayer money, organized a bank-led bail-out of US$3.625 billion. By the end of the fiasco, the total losses were found to be US$4.6 billion.

Case Study 4:

Right before Hungary was slated to be admitted into the European Union (EU), speculators were heavily long the Hungarian forint. This aggressive push upward on the Hungarian currency went counter to the needs and goals of the Hungarian Central Bank (HCM).

One of the HCM's goals in joining the EU was to have their two currencies to converge at 276.1 forints to 1 euro. The aggressive speculation had driven the price of the forint down to 234.69 against the Euro, making their currency so strong that their EU admittance was in jeopardy. The forint had to become weaker in order for Hungary to be admitted to the EU.

The primary speculative culprits were European banks attempting to capitalize on the upward momentum. Their idea was simple: take a long position in the forint and a short position in the euro. They used borrowed money to buy high-yielding Hungarian bonds.

In order to reach their convergence goals, HCM began to aggressively slash interest rates, along with several other macroeconomic intervention techniques, costing speculators approximately US$5 billion.

Summary

While you may draw your own conclusions from each one of these stories, I would hope that you see not only the cautionary side, but also the positive opportunities that mature, overheated, and emerging currencies provide.

Section Two:

Mistakes That Forex Speculators Make

Chapter Six
Leverage is a double-edged sword

Leverage is not an after-thought in the forex market. It is the foundation of the forex industry. In the case studies, we saw how LTCM used $4 billion to leverage over $1 trillion dollars in assets. We saw how George Soros used forex leverage to earn $1 billion dollars against the British pound.

On the other hand, this same forex leverage drove LTCM to the brink of bankruptcy and nearly caused worldwide financial meltdown. We also saw George Soros be hit with a $2 billion dollar loss in the Russian ruble. Forex leverage is not to be taken lightly.

Leverage is defined as "the use of investment capital in such a way that a relatively small amount of money enables the investor to control a relatively large value". In many instances you can have leverage as high as 100:1, sometimes even higher. Putting up a few hundred dollars to have a position worth hundreds of thousands can definitely be worthwhile.

An important fact to remember is that, in both futures and forex, the money used to leverage a position does not have any intrinsic value. The margin is not a deposit on the actual position. Instead it is considered "earnest" money or a "good-faith" deposit . In the case of futures, the margin simply reflects the current volatility and market.

In forex, the margin is a flat rate that helps put you on the playing field. This type of leverage can be terrifying for speculators.

For example, typical OTC leverage rules look like this:

A minimum margin of $1,000 per unit for accounts less than $25,000. Traders must maintain a balance $1,000 or 1% for each open unit. This Alaron FX policy permits you to trade foreign currencies on a highly leveraged basis (up to 100 times your investment). An investment of $1,000 would enable you to trade up to $100,000 of a particular currency. A 50% loss in the value of an account, also known as a "draw down", in usable margin will generate a margin call.

Futures forex leverage is just as bad:

If you trade one Chicago Mercantile Exchange (CME) futures contract on the euro you would effectively be leveraging a total 125,000 euros. The amount of margin you would put up is currently US$3,240. As of this writing, 1 ECU = US$1.20. The US dollar value of this contract is effectively US$150,000. Your margin is only 2.16 % of the total value. Every point movement is the equivalent of $12.50.

If you list yourself as a hedger you can take advantage of "spread margins". A spread margin takes into account that you may have a cash position, or another futures position, in a later month. Therefore, risk and volatility greatly decreases. A spread margin on a euro contract is only US$400. US$400 is only a quarter of 1% of the total face value of the futures contract.

Typically, a speculator new to forex trading will initiate his first trade by getting as many contracts as possible, thereby over-leveraging his account. The greed demon has set in. It is no longer acceptable to just get $7 for every one pip move, it's better to get $70 or maybe $700 for every one pip move.

Unfortunately, this behavior is not discouraged by the majority of brokerages, OTC or futures. Instead, they fuel this greedy behavior. A broker or dealer is paid either on a commission or a pip spread according to the number of contracts his client margins. So it's more profitable for the broker or dealer, at least in the short run, for the client to get as many positions as he can afford to take on margin.

This over-leveraging does a disservice to both the client and the broker. It exposes the client to too much risk at one time and it forces the brokerages to continually get new clients to trade. As a matter of fact, it is not unusual for the first trade a new speculator makes to move against him. Disciplined speculators know to expect that every trade they take may work against them. That being the case, the disciplined speculator paces himself by investing a little at a time until he hits upon a successful trade.

As is to be expected, even the best trading systems that exist rarely have better than a fifty-percent success rate. Therefore, you must let leverage work for you and not allow the demon of greed convince you to abuse it.

Chapter Seven
Confusing speculation with gambling

A few years ago I watched the movie **Rounders.** If you haven't seen it, it is a great movie about poker playing. I immediately became enamored. I then did my research and bought several books on how to play. I also bought some books on game theory, which talked about percentages and odds.

I eventually had the opportunity to play a game of Texas No Limit Hold'em. I was the greenest guy at the table. I am sure that I was pegged for the "mark" right away. Then I got lucky: a pair of Aces on the first hand, Ace King on my second hand, and double Jacks with a Jack on the "flop".

There I was with these guys who had played before, and had won significant money in the past, to hear them tell it. And I was having a case of beginner's luck. I didn't know even a fraction of what these guys knew, nor did I have any experience. Yet there was nothing they could do about it. The situation was out of their control.

This is anecdotal, but it has been my overall experience with gambling. No matter what you know or what you think you know, you have absolutely no control over the situation. You can't analyze the situation and the end results often have no rhyme or reason. You can do everything to better your odds; know a little more statistics, bluff a little better than the next guy, or learn to count cards. Regardless, there is still no accurate way to analyze or predict random occurrences. That's why casinos stay in business and can afford to give away hotel rooms.

One definition of speculation is "the use of money to assume risks for short-term profit, in the knowledge that substantial or total losses are one possible outcome". This is in contrast to gambling, where substantial or total losses are the most likely outcome.

As speculators, we are not creating risk where none existed before, unlike gambling. We are a necessary part of commerce. Not unlike the merchant bankers of old, we are providing the necessary liquidity that allows currencies to smooth out their exchange price for the efficient purchasing of goods and services worldwide.

The bankers and the international conglomerates are in a constant tug-of-war. Each wants access to low interest rates and favorable rates of exchange, either for themselves or their clients. They also want to protect themselves from volatile currency fluctuations that may hurt their bottom line.

Speculation in this type of hostile environment is not for everyone. There are those who want short-term profits but cannot handle the possibility of losing all of the money they have invested. If some of you reading this book have come to this conclusion, I congratulate and respect you. I am quite sure that once you have read this book in its entirety you may just realize that you can handle a potential total loss, so long as you've done everything in your power to prevent it. You too can become a speculator.

Then there are those of you that want the short-term profits. They can handle the possibility of losing all of the money invested in order to boost the overall returns in their investment portfolios. You are speculators.

Then there are those that want the excitement of trading and could care less about the total losses. They just want to be a part of something big. You are not a speculator. You are a gambler. Futures, foreign exchange, or any other derivatives can be an expensive way to learn about your potential addiction. Open your eyes to how the winners speculate. It may encourage you to stick to Atlantic City or Las Vegas.

Chapter Eight
Under-funding a trading account

Approximately 80% of new businesses fail within their first year. The most common problems have been two things: under-capitalization or over-capitalization. As we exit the first wave of the dot com era, we realize that many dot com companies suffered from over-capitalization and were allowed to operate at an unnecessary loss for far too long.

Forex traders suffer from the same two problems. The best way to determine how much to use to fund your account is by considering what market arena you intend to trade in. If you intend to trade OTC forex, you capitalize your account one way. If you intend to trade forex futures, you capatalize it another way. If you want to take advantage of both areas, you capitalize your account in another way still.

Using a total of five to ten percent of your entire stock or mutual fund portfolio is not a bad way to start. On a $100,000 stock portfolio, you should be putting in $10,000. On a $500,000 stock portfolio, you would probably put $25,000 into a managed futures or forex account, and another $25,000 into a self-directed forex account.

If you don't intend to trade both OTC and futures forex, you can get away with smaller amounts. That figure should be no less than

$2,500 and no greater than $50,000 for a self-directed account.

If your net liquid assets are not at least $50,000, but you have $5,000 or less as disposable assets, then you can still speculate in forex. You will use either a mini-cash account or a mini-futures account. If losing your investment would significantly impact your life, DO NOT SPECULATE. No brokerage firm that cares wants that kind of business.

One disturbing trend in the OTC forex investment world is aggressive online marketing, which constantly advertises to novices. Everyone knows that it is difficult to attempt to learn how to trade while trading.

In lieu of giving you one-on-one mentorship, companies that only offer OTC forex, give you demo accounts that trade US$50,000. This is far removed from the typical forex trader's initial account deposit and can actually make the transition to a regular trading account more difficult.

There are a few firms that have combined the OTC forex and futures forex into one division. They have advisors that are well versed in both arenas and capable of helping you avoid common problems. If you find one, work with them. An advisor can be a tremendous help during the early stages, especially when 90% of traders fail. As the adage goes, two heads are better than one. A good advisor can provide the accurate counterbalance and sounding board for the serious speculator.

I know we live in the age of do-it-yourself-ers, but I believe that those who start off trading by themselves are actually lengthening their learning curve. Like any skill, if you develop bad habits in the beginning, it is almost impossible to break them later. The bad habits in trading are succumbing to the demons of fear and greed. Don't fall victim!

Chapter Nine
Commission or no commission

Someone new to forex trading will often times hear that OTC forex has "no commissions". Although there may not be any broker commission charged up front, every transaction has a built in bid/ask spread. This spread can range from five to seven pips , the equivalent of approximately US$35 – US$49. Every time you take a trade, this built in spread shows up.

The way the brokerages make money is by receiving a "rebate" of part of this spread. This "rebate" is equivalent to a commission. As always, there are no free lunches.

When you trade forex futures you may be charged a commission but you don't have to worry about a spread and a back-end rebate.

When it comes to forex trading, don't use the cost of commissions as the linchpin to your trading decision. First, determine your trading style and strategy and then decide what type of brokerage firm you can work with that will accommodate your strategy. As always, don't buy the price; buy the value of the service.

The allure of no commission trading is highly deceptive. If it seems too good to be true, it probably is. This is not to say don't trade OTC forex; just do it for the right reasons. "Commission-free" OTC forex and "commission-based" futures forex can both be used to create success.

Chapter Ten
Churning your own account

Churning is defined as "constantly entering and exiting trades solely to generate commissions". All futures brokers have passed the Series 3 examination and are members of the National Futures Association. They are all regulated and policed by the Commodity Futures Trading Commission and the National Futures Association.

It is written in the rules and regulations of the CFTC that a Series 3 broker must not churn accounts or he will be reprimanded and can face fines and loss of his license. This being the case, it baffles me that small speculators have decided to churn their own accounts, and they have decided to be so bold as to give it a name, "day trading". Any Series 3 broker would lose his job for actively encouraging his clients to trade this way.

Unfortunately, there is no equivalent licensing in the OTC forex market. With the fast-paced, 24-hour nature of forex and the rules that encourage day trading it is difficult not to succumb to the pressure.

If your strategy requires that you day trade, that is fine. Throughout my career though, I have seen more people day trade because of the emotions of fear and greed than from any set strategy.

With forex futures trading, be even more cautious in your attempts at day trading. Currencies, more than any other type of speculation, lend themselves to trending. When a currency makes a fundamental shift, either up or down, it will tend to continue in that direction. Currencies reflect the productivity and capabilities of entire nations. They are slow to move, but once they get started momentum carries them. Don't be afraid to exploit these tendencies in a less aggressive futures account.

If you trade multiple contracts every day, you are doing only one thing: giving money to the brokerage firm. So it is to your benefit to be deliberately entering and exiting trades, not simply churning your account.

For the small speculator, trading conservatively can make all the difference. Depending on your system and the markets traded, you can catch handsome profits by trading a few times a week.

If you set your profit goals before you ever trade, you won't churn your account. Gamblers can't handle that. Speculators know it's true.

Do not let anyone churn your account. That includes you.

Chapter Eleven
Develop a Trading Plan

Why are you trading forex? Why not invest in bonds? Why not buy mutual funds? What is the opportunity cost of not trading forex? Can you stomach potentially losing all of your risk capital? What does risk mean to you? What are your goals for trading forex? Are those goals realistic? How will you attain those goals? How long will you give yourself to attain those goals? Who will help you attain your goals? How much risk capital will you use?

There are many more questions you can ask yourself. These are just a few of the essentials. Like any adventure, you must know what you are in search of, whether it is the Golden Fleece, El Dorado, or the Holy Grail. Once you've defined your quest, you must determine how best to tackle it.

Trading forex can be a most rewarding, exciting experience for the prepared. For the unprepared, it can be a downward spiral like Dante's inferno, becoming more and more painful as you lose more and more money, not knowing exactly why. You will be in trades that could have been profitable had you held on 15 minutes longer, or be the last man into a sure thing only to see it sink like a stone.

A well thought-out trading plan may be no more than two pages but it will be your most vital road map. It will tell you how much you are willing to lose on a trade. It will tell you when to enter a trade, when to exit a trade, and show you how to protect your profits.

Trading forex is easy to get into - probably too easy. If you have the money, almost any brokerage firm will open an account for you. Few brokers will sit down with you to develop a trading plan. This is your responsibility.

Trading forex should be approached like a business. It is a business that anyone can succeed in. The level of your education is immaterial. In fact, the most analytical people have a hard time actually trading and succeeding at speculating. This is because these people are so fixated on developing the perfect system that they forget that it's the trading that counts. Any system will work if you couple it with the discipline that a trading plan brings to the table.

The cliché is that you ride your profits and cut your losses. A trading plan is the cliché brought to life.

Trading Plan Checklist

1. Am I psychologically and financially suited to trade in the futures markets?
2. What are my goals?
3. What are my limitations?
4. How will I keep a trading journal?
5. Will I trade OTC, futures, or options?
6. What currencies will I trade?
7. How will I do my analysis?
8. What trading system will I use?
9. Do I have hard and fast money-management rules?

10. What trading strategies will I use?

11. What type of orders do I plan to use?

12. What do I need from my broker?

Chapter Twelve
Keep a trading journal

The trading journal is the twin to the trading plan. A trading journal tells the story of the trading plan and it creates objectivity. It explains in detail why you took the trade that you did. It also details what your thoughts were at the time of the trade, what your thoughts were during the trade, and what your thoughts were once you were out of the trade. It hopefully eliminates the romanticism of trading and turns you into a speculator.

After a year of keeping a trading journal, you will be able to analyze why you succeeded when you did and why you failed when you did. A full-service broker, like a doctor should be keeping notes on your progress and your state of mind when you are trading.

Without the trading journal to keep you honest, you will not stick to your futures trading plan. Over time, after analyzing the trades in your trading journal, your mind will begin to organize every trade according to a winner's thought process and you will find that the losses won't sting so badly and the wins won't be so surprising.

Chapter Thirteen
Trading by consensus

I am the number one victim of this. When I was trading futures for a living, I would check out every analyst report I could find online to validate my trades. This was in spite of all the indications that my trading plan was giving me. I would sometimes call up my broker friends, or even other full time traders I knew, just to see what they were doing.

I did this for one reason only, I wasn't sure if I should take the trade. Maybe a trade almost met the requirements of my trading plan and I was getting the trading itch. Or maybe I had a couple of losses in a row and was trading with a weak ego. Whatever the case, it was the wrong thing to do. I invariably lost money by hesitating or getting in too early. You name it; I did it…wrong. To this day I can't believe I still have hair because there were weeks, especially in the beginning, when I was literally pulling it out.

Needless to say, don't listen to or ask others about your trades if you want to be a successful trader. The fact is, the best traders are loners. This is very evident in forex trading. There are few, if any analysts, that can successfully take into account every single macroeconomic element that affects a currency. Most of the time, they are shooting in the dark just as much as you are. Your best market decisions will be based on your trading plan, so stick to it until your trade proves or disproves itself. There is no need to allow outside noise to interfere with the precise focus necessary to succeed.

Listening to other people distorts your resolve. It skews your personal interpretation of the data the market is giving you and makes you second-guess yourself, especially if your friends or various analysts agree with you. You can easily fall into the trap of over-thinking your trading.

The funny thing is that there are trading systems based solely on the fact that the crowd is wrong. The market sentiment graph on the Commodity Price Charts, for example, is based on the opinions of analysts. One odd, but telling thing that occurs is that when the market sentiment graph is nearing 100 percent, the market itself is at or near its high. The market sentiment graph doesn't start moving down until after the market has reversed its trend.

The bottom line is that no one knows your trade better than you. Do the trade and let the trade prove itself. Just know that most of the time your trades will fail and there's nothing you can do to change that. The market will do what it wants. You simply want to lose less on the losing trades so that you have enough capital left over to find those potentially winning trades.

Chapter Fourteen
Money Management

This is the last chapter of this section, but it is in no way the least important. In fact, all of the other thirteen chapters are rooted in sound money management techniques. So I now feel comfortable in bringing everything full circle.

Forex speculation is a zero-sum game: the losers give to the winners. All trades are typically settled within 48 hours. That's all she wrote.

There are no guarantees when you are a speculator. There is always the possibility that you will lose all of your risk capital. In fact, I can promise you, and I can't emphasize this enough, YOU WILL HAVE LOSING TRADES. In fact, I can promise that you will have *many* losing trades. So the question I pose to you is, "is the risk worth the potential gain?" Only you can answer that.

Many people have made millions as speculators, and many have lost millions as speculators. The book *Market Wizards* by Jack D. Schwager does a great job of chronicling some of these speculators.

The truth of the matter is that any type of speculating, real estate, futures or other, is similar to batting averages. If you're batting in the 300's that means that out of ten times at bat you've hit the ball three times. You don't know when those three times will occur. They may come all in a row at the beginning or be spread out intermittently among the ten different times at bat. The bottom line is that those three hits can completely make up for, and sometimes overshadow, the seven times you missed at bat. Any one of those hits can represent a grand slam or a double. A true speculator must internalize this concept.

Therefore, a speculator that uses money management must be able to do three things well: be patient, be disciplined, and be frugal. Remember, in forex, unlike many investments, you can afford to be frugal. Often times you have a 100 to 1 leverage ratio on each contract you trade. There is no need to succumb to the demon of greed. Margin one or two contracts at a time and keep the rest in reserve to give your trade an opportunity to prove itself.

Place your stops and map out your exit strategy according to your trading plan. Write down why you took the trade in your trading journal.

If the trade doesn't work out, the stops you have used should have left you capital for the next potential trade. Write down what happened in your journal. Once again, bide your time. When conditions are right again according to your trading plan, put your next trade in. Don't talk to anyone about the trade. Don't look for consensus. Don't allow the demon of fear to hold you back from making your next trade. Make the trade and write down why you took it.

The cycle repeats itself. After a year of this deliberate trading, measure your overall return on investment and determine if trading forex was worth it for you. Anything less than a year's worth of effort and energy put into forex speculation is both unfair to the speculator and unfair to this type of investing.

In everything in life, there is a healthy type of fear that exists. It is called respect. You must respect the forex market. Like the ocean, it is vast and the waves of profit and loss obey their own rhythm. Your little $5,000, $50,000, or even $500,000 doesn't affect the market in any way. We are talking about an industry that trades US$1.5 trillion dollars daily. Your money is your boat and, like any intelligent sailor that wants to arrive at his destination, you must plan in advance (trading plan), and take a log of what happens (trading journal), and only deviate when the *market* tells you to deviate.

You are at the mercy of the market; you can ride the currents or fight against them. I have to say though, if I were a gambling man, my money is with those who go along for the ride.

Section Three:

Forex Trading Arenas

Chapter Fifteen
Over The Counter (OTC) Market

Forex trading falls into two arenas, OTC and Futures. This schism developed early on. Banks developed the OTC market as a way to provide added-value services to their large multinational clients. OTC forex is oftentimes considered to be spot/cash transactions. In the beginning, these spot transactions were considered essential for multinational corporations to operate efficiently.

The banks also considered OTC forex to be a risk-free way of generating profits. The same way that LTCM saw narrowing spreads between bonds as risk free capital, banks consider the spreads between currency bid and ask prices free money. Banks fought to make sure that foreign currency exchange was seen as an express power of banking with no need for additional regulatory oversight. With such an aggressive stance by the banks, the OTC markets' explosive growth was inevitable.

While much of foreign exchange trading could have been conducted on the regulated exchanges, the banks didn't support it and created their own instruments as substitutes. OTC forex has expanded from its early roots as a spot transaction market. Over US$1.5 trillion is traded daily. Independent dealers now out number banks in offering OTC currencies.

Participants

There are 93 major players in the forex market in the United States. Many of these are subsidiaries of foreign banks. Some are investment banks or insurance firms, but most are based in New York.

The total volume of transactions of the *reporting* dealers among themselves account for $500 billion - $750 billion + per day. On any given day their activity can account for almost half, if not more, of all the OTC forex activity.

Central banks worldwide have a heavy hand in the foreign exchange market as well. They use it to regulate their economy. Yet, as we have seen in the case study regarding the Bank of England, even with their purchasing power they could not stop the collapse of the British pound.

Instruments

Spot : Settled two days after deal date

Pre-Spot: Settled one day after deal date

Pre-Spot "Cash": Settled immediately

FX Swap: one spot transaction plus one forward transaction

Currency Swap: the exchange of principal in two different currencies at the beginning and a re-exchange of same amount at the end.

Currency Forwards: Customized contracts for future delivery of currency.

Currency options: Customized contracts that grant the right, but not the obligation to exchange a fixed amount of currency at or before a fixed time in the future.

OTC forex trading

OTC forex trading focuses primarily on the following movers: US dollar, British pound, euro, Japanese yen, and Swiss franc. These currencies are the most actively traded in the world and are known as the "hard" currencies. Since currencies are traded in pairs, the following hard currency pairs account for 80% of all OTC trading.

USD/EUR

USD/JPY

GBP/USD

USD/SFR

EUR/YEN

EUR/GBP

Other currencies not listed here are considered soft currencies. There are approximately 34 soft currencies traded.

Advantages

1. 24-hour market
2. Margin ability of up to 500:1 leverage
3. US$1.5 trillion traded daily. Three times larger than the worldwidestock and bond markets combined
4. No overt commissions
5. Price is negotiated

Disadvantages

1.24-hour market

2.Easy to over-leverage

3.No centralized market place

4.Interest charges for holding a position too long

5.Price knowledge is limited to your dealer

Trading Tips

1. 24-hour market - Trade only on major announcements or reports

2. Trading time- frames: 15- minute and 60- minute

3. Use US Dollar Index (USDX) as a guide

   a. the US Dollar Index is a composition of all major currencies.

   b. Strength or weakness can give you an idea of where your
      cash position will go.

4. Futures counterparts can provide crucial information:

   a. Front month trades closely to cash

   b. Volume

   c. Open Interest

   d. Commitment of Trader's Report

   e. General technical indicators

Chapter Sixteen
Exchange Traded Arenas

There are three exchange-traded markets: the Chicago Mercantile Exchange, the New York Board of Trade, and the Philadelphia Stock Exchange.

Each of these exchange-traded markets has their own history of development. In this chapter we will briefly synopsize each exchange. Hopefully you will gain some insight into how they came about, who they are, and what they trade.

Participants:

The exchange-traded markets are dominated by only two groups:

Hedgers – The same banks and dealers that carry cash positions in the interbank market will use futures contracts to protect themselves from over exposure to trades, and

Speculators- Those that want to profit from the price discrepancy between hedgers. They provide the capital liquidity that the exchange traded foreign exchange markets need to operate properly.

Advantages

1. Exchanges have transparency
2. Guaranteed counterparty system

3. Accurate volume and open interest figures

4. No bid/ask spread

5. Able to hold position trades

Disadvantages

1. Most active during Central and Eastern Standard times

2. Significantly less liquidity than the cash forex market

3. Margins are typically 2% of the contract value (50:1)

4. Commission

5. Exchange does not reflect all of the various foreign exchange trading

Commodity Exchanges

Chicago Mercantile Exchange (CME)

When the CME launched currency futures in 1972, it was the world's first financial futures contract. Prior to this, the CME only traded commodities, such as corn, wheat, and pork bellies. This new development was in direct response to the breakdown of the Bretton Woods Agreement.

On May 16, 1972, seven forex currency futures contracts were listed. They were British pounds, Canadian dollars, Deutsche marks, French francs, Japanese yen, Mexican pesos and Swiss francs.

In April 2001, CME expanded FX market coverage by offering electronic access to its full range of currency contracts virtually 24 hours a day via the GLOBEX electronic trading platform. This electronic trading access functions "side-by-side" with floor trading in CME's currency pits during floor trading hours.

In March 2003, the total notional value of FX trading at CME was US$347.5 billion. Currency futures are derivatives on the inter-bank cash and forward exchange rates.

CME contracts
Australian dollar

Brazilian real

British pounds

Canadian dollars

Euro

French franc

Japanese yen

Mexican peso

Russian ruble

Swiss franc

CME E-mini contracts-
Euro

Japanese yen

New York Board of Trade: Finex Division

The New York Board of Trade currency and options division, Finex, was established in 1985. Their most important contribution to the currency-trading world was their introduction of the US Dollar Index (USDX). The USDX is a basket of the most actively traded currencies and how they relate to the US dollar aggregately.

In 1994, they added currency cross-rates. They also became the first exchange to provide trading floors on two continents with two separate facilities, one location in New York and the second in Dublin, Ireland.

Besides offering a contract on the US Dollar Index, they also trade a total of 29 currency pairs.

Finex- most active contracts

US Dollar Index

Swiss franc/J.yen

Swiss franc/B. pound

J. yen/B. pound

J. yen/Euro

Philadelphia Stock Exchange

The Philadelphia Stock Exchange (PHLX) was founded in 1790 as the first organized stock exchange in the United States. In 1982, PHLX pioneered options on currencies.

Their philosophy was simple; while customized forward contracts and futures markets provide a way to protect yourself from currency fluctuations, options could provide protection without the obligations that came with forward and futures contracts. This was an important shift in ideology for hedgers that were once confined only to the OTC market.

PHLX is the world's leading marketplace for exchange traded currency options because of their versatility. Since they offer both customized and standardized currency options, hedgers are able to tailor the options to their specific needs.

PHLX limits its option trading primarily to the G7 nations. Currently, options are available on the following currencies,: Australian dollar, British pound, Canadian dollar, euro, Japanese yen, Mexican peso, Swiss franc, and U.S. dollar.

Tips to trading exchange forex

1) Cash and Futures Convergence – watch the cash market as futures contracts expire. There may be opportunities to trade the narrowing spread between the two for arbitrage-type profits.

2) Trade cash and futures currencies in a spread position and benefit from the less expensive margins.

3) Potentially use futures as a way to protect your long-term OTC positions.

4) Write options on futures against your OTC positions

5) Understand normal markets and backwardation markets

6) Take advantage of longer term trending

7) Focus your trading mainly in the Chicago Mercantile Exchange

Chapter Seventeen
Conclusion

After being involved with speculative investing for almost eleven years, I hope my experiences as both a broker and a small speculator will benefit you. By no stretch of the imagination is this book going to make you an expert trader. There are no long-lost secrets to reveal, nor are there sure-fire trades to win every time. Although we all wish for these things, anyone promising them is suspect.

I hope that I have provided you with solidly interesting information, without the unnecessary hype. The forex markets have more than enough excitement on their own, without embellishment. As always, truth is stranger than fiction. My primary goal is to make you a more conscientious speculator.

There has yet to be a perfect system, but there are successful, disciplined traders. To be successful you must realize that you have no control over the markets. Nothing you do matters to the market.

Once you accept that, you can turn your focus inward. There you will find two foes: the demons of fear and greed. It is impossible to remove them from your life entirely, but they can be managed. Once you have them under control using a trading plan and a trading journal, you will have brought a sense of security to your trading.

You now know exactly what you are going to do, how you're going to do it, and when you are going to do it.

This is what our motto "Bringing security to speculative investing" means. I wish this for every small speculator.

Good fortune to all of you in your currency trading endeavors.

APPENDIX

Appendix One:
Managed Forex

Managed forex, OTC or futures, are the "mutual funds" of the futures industry. A Commodity Trading Advisor (CTA) manages private investor money and uses various strategies to attempt to minimize the speculative risks associated with futures.

Managed futures are the perfect investment for those who cannot take the time out of their day to follow the markets. It is also appropriate for investors with a large portfolio that are seeking true diversification.

Futures and forex are not correlated to stocks. Any movement, up or down, in the stock market has no bearing on your futures accounts. Investors can put a small portion of their money in futures and actually increase their overall rates of return.

A simple strategy is to take five to ten percent out of your stock portfolio and place it into managed futures and/or forex. This reduces your portfolio volatility and stabilizes returns.

Unfortunately, to set up a managed future or forex account you may need to invest fifty to one hundred thousand dollars ($50,000 - $100,000) or more. Sometimes you can indirectly invest in a managed futures or forex account by participating in a commodity pool. Many commodity pools have smaller minimums. There is no uniformity on how commodity pools or managed futures accounts are run.

It is best to have a prospectus sent to you and have your futures broker or other professional go over the details with you.

Appendix Two:
Forex Glossary

These definitions have been comprised from AlaronFX's website. They are one of the premier OTC forex dealers in the country.

Appreciation

A currency is said to 'appreciate' when it strengthens in price in response to market demand.

Arbitrage

The purchase or sale of an instrument and simultaneous taking of an equal and opposite position in a related market, in order to take advantage of small price differentials between markets.

Around

Dealer jargon used in quoting when the forward premium/discount is near parity. For example, "two-two around" would translate into 2 points to either side of the present spot.

Ask Rate

The rate at which a financial instrument is quoted for sale (as in bid/ ask spread).

Balance of Trade

The value of a country's exports minus its imports.

Base Currency

In general terms, the base currency is the currency in which an investor or issuer maintains its book of accounts. In the FX markets, the US Dollar is normally considered the 'base' currency for quotes, meaning that quotes are expressed as a unit of $1 USD per the other currency quoted in the pair. The primary exceptions to this rule are the British pound, the euro and the Australian dollar.

Bid Rate

The quoted rate at which a trader is willing to buy a currency.

Bid/Ask Spread

The difference between the bid and offer
price, and the most widely used measure of market liquidity.

Big Figure

Dealer expression referring to the first few digits of an exchange rate. These digits rarely change in normal market fluctuations, and therefore are omitted in dealer quotes, especially in times of high market activity. For example, a USD/Yen rate might be 107.30/107.35, but would be quoted verbally without the first three digits i.e. 30/35

Book

In a professional trading environment, a 'book' is the summary of a trader's or desk's total positions.

Bps

Digits added to or subtracted from the fourth decimal place, i.e. 0.0001 or a percent of a percent. Also called Points.

Broker

An individual or firm that acts as an intermediary, matching buyers and sellers (or buy orders and sell orders) for a fee, or commission. In contrast, a 'dealer' commits capital and takes one side of a position, hoping to earn a spread (profit) by closing out the position in a subsequent trade with another party.

Bretton Woods Agreement of 1944

An agreement that established fixed foreign exchange rates for major currencies (pegged against the US dollar), provided for central bank intervention in the currency markets, and pegged the price of gold at US $35 per ounce. The agreement lasted until 1971, when President Nixon overturned the Bretton Woods agreement and established a floating exchange rate for major currencies.

Cable

Trader jargon referring to the Sterling/US Dollar exchange rate. So called because the rate was originally transmitted via a trans-Atlantic cable beginning in the mid 1800's.

Central Bank

A government or quasi-governmental organization that manages a country's monetary policy. For example, the US central bank is the Federal Reserve and the German central bank is the Bundesbank.

Contagion

The tendency of an economic crisis to spread from one market to another. In 1997, political instability in Indonesia caused high volatility in their domestic currency, the rupiah. From there, the contagion spread to other Asian emerging currencies, and then to Latin America. This is now referred to as the 'Asian Contagion'.

Commission

A transaction fee charged by a broker.

Contract

The standard unit of trading.

Counterparty

One of the participants in a financial transaction.

Country Risk

Risk associated with a cross-border transaction, including but not limited to legal and political conditions.

Cross Rate

The exchange rate between any two currencies

that are considered non-standard in the country where the currency pair is quoted. For example, in the US, a GBP/JPY quote would be considered a cross rate, whereas in UK or Japan it would be one of the primary currency pairs traded.

Currency
Any form of money issued by a government or central bank and used as legal tender and a basis for trade.

Currency Risk
The probability of an adverse change in exchange rates.

Day Trading
Refers to the process of taking positions which are opened and closed on the same trading day.

Dealer
An individual who acts as a principal or counterparty to a transaction. Principals take one side of a position, hoping to earn a spread (profit) by closing out the position in a subsequent trade with another party. In contrast, a broker is an individual or firm that acts as an intermediary, matches buyers and sellers (or buy orders and sell orders) for a fee or commission.

Deficit
A negative balance of trade or payments.

Delivery

An FX trade where both sides make and take actual delivery of the currencies traded.

Depreciation

A fall in the value of a currency due to market forces.

Derivative

A contract that changes in value in relation to the price movements of a related or underlying security, future or other physical instrument. An Option is the most common derivative instrument.

Devaluation

The deliberate downward adjustment of a currency's price, normally by official announcement.

Economic Indicator

A government-issued statistic that indicates current economic growth and stability. Common indicators include employment rates, Gross Domestic Product (GDP), inflation, retail sales, etc.

European Monetary Union (EMU)

The principal goal of EMU is to establish a single European currency called the euro, which will officially replaces the national currencies of the member EU countries, with the notable exception of Britain's pound. On Janaury 1, 1999 the transitional phase to introduce the euro began. The euro now exists as a banking currency and paper financial transactions and foreign exchange are made in euros. This transition period will last for three years, at which time euro notes and coins will enter circulation. On July 1, 2002, only euros will be legal tender for EMU participants, the national currencies of the member countries will cease to exist. The current members of the EMU are Germany, France, Belgium, Luxembourg, Austria, Finland, Ireland, the Netherlands, Italy, Spain and Portugal.

Euro

The currency of the Eurozone. A replacement for the European Currency Unit (ECU).

Flat/Square

Dealer jargon used to describe a position that has been completely reversed, e.g. you bought $500,000 then sold $500,000, thereby creating a neutral (flat) position.

Foreign Exchange - (Forex, FX)

The simultaneous buying of one currency and selling of another.

Forward

The pre-specified exchange rate for a foreign exchange contract settling at some agreed future date, based upon the interest rate differential between the two currencies involved.

Forward Points

The bps added to or subtracted from the current exchange rate to calculate a forward price.

Fundamental Analysis

Analysis of economic and political information with the objective of determining future movements in a financial market.

Futures Contract

An obligation to exchange a good or instrument at a set price on a future date. The primary difference between a Future and a Forward is that Futures are typically traded over an exchange (Exchange-Traded Contracts - ETC), versus forwards, which are considered Over The Counter (OTC) contracts. An OTC is any contract NOT traded on an exchange.

Hedge

A position or combination of positions that reduces the risk of your primary position.

Inflation

An economic condition whereby prices for consumer goods rise, eroding purchasing power.

Initial Margin

The initial deposit of collateral required to enter into a position as a guarantee on future performance.

Inter-bank Rates

The foreign exchange rates at which large, international banks quote other large, international banks.

Leading Indicators

Statistics that are considered to predict future economic activity.

LIBOR

The London Inter-Bank Offered Rate. Banks use LIBOR when borrowing from another bank.

Limit Order

An order with restrictions on the maximum price to be paid or the minimum price to be received. As an example, if the current price of USD/YEN is 102.00/05, then a limit order to buy USD would be at a price below 102. (ie 101.50)

Liquidation

The closing of an existing position through the execution of an offsetting transaction.

Long Position

A position that appreciates in value if market prices increase.

Margin

The required equity that an investor must deposit to collateralize a position.

Margin Call

A request from a broker or dealer for additional funds or other collateral to guarantee performance on a position that has moved
 against the customer.

Market Maker

A dealer who regularly quotes both bid and ask prices and is ready to make a two-sided market (buy or sell) for a given financial instrument.

Market Risk

Exposure to changes in market prices.

Mark-to-Market

Process of re-evaluating all open positions with the current market prices. These new values then determine margin requirements.

Maturity

The date for settlement or expiry of a financial instrument.

Offer

The rate at which a dealer is willing to sell a currency.

Offsetting Transaction

A trade which serves to cancel or offset some or all of the market risk of an open position.

Over the Counter (OTC)

Used to describe any transaction that is not conducted over an exchange.

Overnight

A trade that remains open until the next business day.

Pips

Digits added to or subtracted from the fourth decimal place, i.e. 0.0001. Also called Basis Points.

Political Risk

Exposure to changes in government policy that will have an adverse effect on an investor's position.

Premium

In the currency markets, describes the amount by which the forward or futures price exceed the spot price.

Rate

The price of one currency in terms of another, typically used for dealing purposes.

Revaluation

An increase in the exchange rate for a currency as a result of central bank intervention. Opposite of Devaluation.

Risk

Exposure to uncertain change, most often used with a negative connotation of adverse change.

Risk Management

The employment of financial analysis and trading techniques to reduce and/or control exposure to various types of risk.

Roll-Over

Process whereby the settlement of a deal is rolled forward to another value date . The cost of this process is based on the interest rate differential of the two currencies.

Settlement

The process by which a trade is entered into the books and records of the counterparts to a transaction. The settlement of currency trades may or may not involve the actual physical exchange of one currency for another.

Short Position

An investment position that benefits from a decline in market price.

Spot Price

The current market price. Settlement of spot transactions usually occurs within two business days.

Sterling (or Pound Sterling)

Slang for British Pound.

Stop Loss Order

Order type whereby an open position is automatically liquidated at a specific price. Often used to minimize exposure to losses if the market moves against an investor's position. As an example, if an investor is long USD at 156.27, they might wish to put in a stop loss order for 155.49, which would limit losses should the dollar depreciate, possibly below 155.49.

Swap

A currency swap is the simultaneous sale and purchase of the same amount of a given currency at a forward exchange rate.

Tomorrow Next (Tom/Next)

Simultaneous buying and selling of a currency for delivery the following day.

Turnover

The total monetary value of all executed transactions in a given time period; volume.

Two-Way Price

When both a bid and offer rate is quoted for a FX transaction.

Uptick

A new price quote at a price higher than the preceding quote.

US Prime Rate

The interest rate at which US banks will lend to their prime corporate customers.

Yard

Slang for a billion.

Enlightened Financial Press
Mail, fax, or website:

Enlightened Financial Press
404 E. First St. Suite 1396, Long Beach, CA 90802

Fax: 1-509-461-5864 Web: www.smallspeculators.com

ITEM	TITLE	PRICE EACH	QUANTITY	TOTAL
BOOK	Futures For Small Speculators	$19.95		
BOOK	Forex For Small Speculators	$19.95		
BOOK	Futures For Small Speculators: Companion Guide	$24.95		
BOOK	Single Stock Futures For Small Speculators: The complete guide	$24.95		
SPECIALTY	Futures For Small Speculators Newsletter	$97/year		
SPECIALTY	Futures For Small Speculators Weekly Trade Alert	$287/year		
TELEPHONE SEMINAR	Futures For Small Speculators- E-mail to find out current topic	$87.00		
PRIVATE CONSULTATION	1 hour consultation with the author Noble A. DraKoln	$250/hr		
TOTAL PACKAGE	Every thing listed above plus 1 hour of consultation every week for a month.	$1250		

Make Money Orders or Checks payable to:
Enlightened Financial Press

Shipping Costs: (shipping double outside of USA)

$0-$5.00	$3.50	$25.00-$50.00	$6.50
$5.01-$15.00	$4.50	$50.01-$100.00	$7.50
$15.01-$25.00	$5.50	$100.01 or more	$9.50

Name: —————————————————— Date: —————

Email: ————————————————

Address:

———————————————————————————

———————————————————————————

City: ——————————————State: —————Zip:—————

Country: ——————————————

Phone: ————————————Work Phone:

Shipping address: (if different from above)

———————————————————————————

———————————————————————————

City: ————————————State: ————————————

Zip: ————————————

Payment: Check ——————————Money Order ————————————

Through "PayPal.Com" we accept Visa, Master Card, and Direct Debit.Send payment to billing@liverpoolgroup.com

Contact us directly for questions about bulk orders

+1 562-434-4791